THE RISE OF RASTAFARI

Resistance, Redemption & Repatriation

Makonnen Sankofa

Published by

PEACHES

PUBLICATIONS

Published in London, United Kingdom by
Peaches Publications, 2019.
www.peachespublications.co.uk

British Library Cataloging in Publication Data
A catalogue record for this book is available
from the British Library.

ISBN: 9781515366430

Book cover design: Peaches Publications

Typesetter: Winsome Duncan

CONTENTS

DEDICATION

This book is dedicated to the founders and early followers of Rastafari. These men and women devoted their lives for the liberation of black people and they defended Rastafari despite facing severe discrimination from government authorities and the society at the time. Thanks and praises to the founding fathers of the Rastafari Movement. These men are Leonard Howell, Joseph Hibbert, Archibald Dunkley, and Robert Hinds.

ACKNOWLEDGEMENTS

I give special acknowledgment to Mutabaruka in writing this book. Mutabaruka is a Rastafarian elder, radio talk show host and dub poet. Mutabaruka has inspired me throughout my journey of Rastafari and his work has influenced me to write this book.

INTRODUCTION

Rastafari has taken the world by storm. You can travel to different continents around the world and you will find Rastafarians. However, the perception of what people think Rastafari is will differ depending on who you speak to and where you go. Therefore, Rastafari is one of the most misunderstood groups in the world. Even many followers of Rastafari, don't have a correct understanding of the movement. Myself being a devout Rastafarian, I wanted to write a book that would educate people so they can get a true understanding of what Rastafari is.

I first got interested in Rastafari through roots reggae music. When I listened to reggae music and kept hearing the reggae artists sing about Haile Selassie I, I was curious and interested to find out more about this man. So I bought *The*

Autobiography of Emperor Haile Selassie I, Volume 1. I also watched some documentaries about Emperor Haile Selassie I. After reading parts of *The Autobiography of Emperor Haile Selassie I, Volume 1* and watching the documentaries, I wanted to know more about Haile Selassie I and the Rastafari Movement. So I started studying Rastafari. I acquired information from various sources which included books, documentaries, lectures, interviews, music songs, writings, going to Rastafari events, and having discussions with Rastafarians.

I was attracted to the black liberation theology of Rastafari. Rastafari appealed to me because it was relevant to my history as someone from African-Caribbean heritage and it offered me an identity, culture and spirituality from an African perspective. I initially identified with Haile Selassie I because he was a black king who looked like me. When I was younger, whether at school or outside school; I only heard about white kings and queens until I came across Haile Selassie I. The more interested I got into Rastafari, the more I found out about Haile Selassie I. I admire Haile Selassie I as someone who did a lot of great things to help Africa and African people at a crucial time in world history.

Most people when they think of Rastafari,

the first things that come to their minds are dreadlocks, smoking ganja and vegetarianism. It is a travesty that Rastafari is often thought of in this way because it completely disregards the true essence of what Rastafari is. Rastafari is much more than just a culture. The key element of the Rastafari Movement is Pan-Africanism. Brother Leader Mbandaka is the founder and leader of the Alkebulan Revivalist Movement, which is a Pan-African organisation inspired by Rastafari. Brother Leader Mbandaka said: "It is important that we realise that to be a true Rasta, is to be a Pan-Africanist. You cannot separate Rastafari and Pan-Africanism, if we understand the root and the origin of Rastafari." (Brother Leader Mbandaka's speech can be accessed on YouTube web page: www.youtube.com/watch?v=imBRAGpYPwE. Acccessed on 12 March 2019).

A lot of Rastafarians get caught up in validating Haile Selassie I through the Bible. So they have turned a Pan-African movement into a religion where you see Rastafarians set up churches, tabernacles and read the Bible. I don't regard Haile Selassie I as the creator of the universe. I don't acknowledge Haile Selassie I as someone who makes miracles happen. Neither do I believe that Haile Selassie I is the reincarnation of Jesus Christ. I don't refer to Haile

Selassie I using the term God because most people's understanding of God is influenced by religious books where God is the creator of the universe. Merriam-Webster's online dictionary states that there are many different terms for God.

"1: [God] The supreme or ultimate reality: such as

a: [God] The being perfect in power, wisdom, and who is worshipped as creator and ruler of the universe.

b: The incorporeal divine principle ruling over all as eternal Spirit: infinite mind.

2: [God] A being or object believed to have more than natural attributes and powers and to require human worship.

3: [God] A person or thing of supreme value.

4: [God] A powerful ruler."

(The definitions of God were taken from the Merriam-Webster online dictionary web page: www.merriam-webster.com/dictionary/god. Accessed on 12 March 2019).

I would certainly refer to Haile Selassie I as a God based on the definitions given in point 3 and point 4 (above in the Merriam-Webster dictionary) but not as a God as defined in point

1 or 2 from the Merriam-Webster dictionary. In ancient times, the Egyptians worshiped the Pharaohs (monarchs) as man, ruler and God. The concept of Rastafari is very similar, it is to see God in the physical manifestation of man. We have created our own living God in Haile Selassie I and we acknowledge him as a man, ruler (king) and God. We don't need to validate Haile Selassie I through the Bible to come to this conclusion. Instead, we must praise Haile Selassie I for the role he has played in trying to liberate Africa. We must also recognise the significance of Haile Selassie I being the only Emperor of an independent African country during the 19th century colonial era, when European nations controlled most of the continent. Haile Selassie I showed the world that a black man can run a country successfully, at a time where the nations of Europe believed that African people where uncivilised and incapable of running their own country by themselves.

As Rastafarians, we do not seek our reward in heaven after we die. Instead, we strive for a better life for black people on earth today and for our future generations. And we strive for this, in the name of a black king, in a black country (in Africa), which is run and ruled by black people, without negative influences from the West and

Arabs, who have caused destruction to Africa and African people in the past and present.

WHAT IS RASTAFARI?

Rastafari is a Pan-African movement that is aimed at the uplift of black people: spiritually, culturally, politically, and economically. Rastafari is about liberating the minds of black people because we have been taught to think bad about ourselves, due to subjugation and brainwashing that has been imposed on us over the last five hundred years, which has come from slavery, colonialism, neo-colonialism and cultural imperialism.

Rastafarians regard the Ethiopian Emperor Haile Selassie I as either an idol, God or the reincarnation of Jesus Christ. Rastafarians declare Marcus Garvey (Jamaica's first National Hero) as a prophet who has guided black people towards Ethiopia/Africa to a black king to help liberate them from the unjust system of white supremacy which has been oppressing black people.

Rastafari philosophy is based on the Pan-African teachings of Marcus Garvey (see points bullet below).

- Self-reliance of the black race.
- Unity amongst black people.
- Putting the best interests of the black race first.
- Building a strong black nation.
- Repatriation to Africa.
- Acknowledging divinity within our own race.

In the late 1920s, Marcus Garvey prophesied the crowning of an African king to be the liberator of black people. Shortly after this, Haile Selassie I became king of Ethiopia. Then 2 years later, Haile Selassie I became Emperor of Ethiopia in 1930. Following the coronation of Haile Selassie I as Emperor of Ethiopia, Leonard Howell (a ex-member of Marcus Garvey's Universal Negro Improvement Association) started preaching in Jamaica that Haile Selassie I is the only ruler for black people. Jamaica is a significant place, not only because its where Rastafari began but because the majority of the population in Jamaica are descendants of African slaves who were brought there during the transatlantic slave trade. Jamaica is also significant because

Marcus Garvey was born there.

During the 1930s when Rastafari began, there were a few other people that were also preaching about Haile Selassie I independent of Leonard Howell. These men were Archibald Dunkley, Joseph Hibbert and Robert Hinds. The early founders and followers of Rastafari were influenced by literature such as *The Holy Pipy* (often referred to as "The Black Man's Bible") and *The Royal Parchment Scroll of Black Supremacy*. These documents directed black people to look towards Ethiopia/Africa for their liberation. Leonard Howell was the most known out of the four early preachers of Rastafari and Leonard Howell also had the largest number of followers. Leonard Howell is often accredited to being "The first Rasta". The followers of Leonard Howell were called "Howellites".

The three most popular groups within Rastafari today were formed after the original Rastafarians. These three groups (also referred to as mansions) are known as Nyahbinghi, Bobo Shanti and Twelve Tribes of Israel. The oldest group out of these three groups is the Nyahbinghi. The Nyahbinghi group is named after Queen Nyabinghi. She was a warrior queen from Uganda who fought against European colonialism. Nyahbinghi worship Haile Selassie I as God and they hold spiritual gatherings amongst themselves. At these gatherings, there is drumming and chanting that takes place. They call these gatherings "Binghi".

Another Rastafari group is the Bobo Shanti, who are also known as the Bobo Dread. The Bobo Shanti was formed in the 1950s by Charles Edwards. The Bobo Shanti followers call their leader Charles Edwards, "Holy Emmanuel". They believe in a holy trinity, in which Haile Selassie I is God, Marcus Garvey is a prophet and Charles Edwards has been divinely selected as a high priest. The Bobo Shanti claim that they are descendants of the Ashanti (Asante) tribe in Ghana, who were taken to the West Indies during the transatlantic slave trade. The Ashanti are a subgroup within the Akan people of Ghana.

Twelve Tribes of Israel is another Rastafari group. They believe Haile Selassie I is the reincarnation of Jesus Christ and that they are descendants of the twelve lost tribes of Israel that are mentioned in the Bible. Twelve Tribes of Israel was formed by Vernon Carrington in the late 1960s. Vernon Carrington is known as "Prophet Gad" by his followers because he claimed to be the reincarnation of the prophet Gad from the Bible. According to the Bible, the tribe of Gad is one of the twelve tribes of Israel.

Despite there being several groups in Rastafari, there are a lot of Rastafarians who are not part of any specific Rastafari group.

It is common to see Rastafarians with the dreadlocks hairstyle. A person does not have to have dreadlocks to be a Rastafarian. Neither is someone a more devout Rastafarian because they have dreadlocks. It wasn't even common for Rastafarians to style their hair in dreadlocks until the mid-1950s, when Rastafarians decided to adopt the dreadlocks hairstyle from the Mau Mau warriors in Kenya, who were fighting against the British army to gain independence.

Many Rastafarians have a vegetarian based diet known as Ital. The Ital diet came about as a lot of Rastafarians farmed because they lived in rural places and secluded areas in the hills of Jamaica. Rastafarians would grow their own food on their land and eat it. Though there are interpretations of Ital regarding specific foods that differ, the general principle is that food should be natural or pure, and from the earth. Members of the Bobo Shanti and Nyahbinghi are not permitted to eat meat. The Howellites were not known to be vegetarians. Twelve Tribes of Israel followers are permitted to eat meat. A Rastafarian's diet is based on the group that the person belongs to. If a Rastafarian is not part of any specific Rastafari group, then it is up to the individual to decide whether to eat meat or not to eat meat.

Rastafari colours are red, gold (sometimes substituted for yellow) and green. Red represents the blood of African people, gold represents the gold that comes from the land of Africa, and green represents the land of Africa. Rastafarians have adopted the old Ethiopian national flag as their flag. The flag Rastafarians use was the national flag of Ethiopia when Haile Selassie I ruled the country.

One of the main principles of Rastafari is repatriation to Africa. Rastafarians want to go back to Africa because it is the land where our ancestors lived in harmony and built great civilisations before they were kidnapped and forcibly taken to other parts of the world during the transatlantic slave trade. And since our ancestors arrived in other parts of the world against their own will, black people have faced racial oppression over the last five hundred years. Rastafarians want to repatriate to Africa so they can live in peace and help rebuild Africa, following the destruction of African civilisations which has been caused by slavery, colonialism and neo-colonialism.

Ethiopia is important to Rastafarians because

it is the country that Haile Selassie I ruled as Emperor. Ethiopia is also important to the Rastafarians because they regard Ethiopia as a place which symbolises freedom. This is down to the fact that Ethiopia is the only African country that has never been colonised. In 1948, Haile Selassie I donated five hundred acres of his own private land in Shashamane, Ethiopia to the Ethiopian World Federation so that Rastafarians and other black people living in the diaspora could repatriate to Africa. There is a community of Rastafarians living together in Shashamane that is made up of Rastafarians who have relocated from different countries around the world. Many Rastafarians travel to Shashamane or other places within Ethiopia on a pilgrimage at some point in their life. There are also Rastafarians who have repatriated to other parts of Africa, or they have visited at least one of the 54 countries in Africa on holiday.

THE TRANSATLANTIC SLAVE TRADE

The transatlantic slave trade took place between the 15th and 19th centuries. Millions of black Africans were kidnapped by white Europeans or by other Africans on behalf of Europeans. Africans were captured from countries along the west coast of Africa. Europeans could easily access the west coast of Africa by travelling across the Atlantic Ocean.

Some Africans co-operated with the white Europeans to trade other Africans in exchange for goods, which often included weaponry. Africans traded other Africans who were their enemies, prisoners of war, or warriors who belonged to rival tribes. Africans who traded slaves with the Europeans benefited from it, particularly African chiefs who acquired a lot of wealth from trading with the Europeans. Europeans also got hold of African people by forcing Africans who had less weaponry than them to capture other Africans by threatening to enslave the Africans who didn't do as they were told. A small number of Africans were captured by Europeans who came onto land from the west coast of Africa. There was a lot of resistance from Africans who tried to prevent themselves and others from being captured.

After the Africans had been captured, the Africans were forced onto ships and transported to the Caribbean once the Europeans decided they had enough slaves on board. In some cases, slaves were kept in slave fortresses where they were locked up and held for months before they were shipped to the Caribbean. The conditions in these slave fortresses and on the ships were terrible. Africans were kept in the basement of the ships and they were packed closely next to each other with little room to move and chains attached to their hands and feet. Many Africans died on the slave ships because of the bad conditions. Some Africans decided to commit suicide by throwing themselves off the boat into the sea. There was resistance on the slave ships from Africans who fought to be free. But these attempts were often suppressed by the Europeans, who had weaponry such as guns and swords.

Once the Africans arrived in the West Indies, they were turned into slaves who were forced to work on plantations for white slave owners. These Africans were legal property of their slave masters. Slave treatment could differ depending on the slave owners. But in general, the treatment of slaves on plantations was brutal. Field slaves would carry out tasks such as picking sugarcanes, extracting the sugar from sugarcanes, and boiling the sugarcanes to produce juice. These tasks would be carried out from early morning till night. Slaves were not paid any money and they could be beaten if they didn't perform their tasks to the standards that their master or overseer expected of them. If a slave did something their master thought was bad, a slave would be punished based on the judgment of the slave master. Slaves faced brutal punishments, such as being beaten up, having parts of their body cut off, being shot dead, being hanged, or being burned alive. It was common for female slaves to be raped by their masters, even though these women didn't do anything wrong. If a master desired a slave woman, he would rape her; even if she was married.

Slaves were stripped of their identity, culture and beliefs. Slaves were forced to adopt a new name, a new language to speak and a new God to worship. Families were separated when slaves were sold by their masters. The children of the African slaves were born into slavery and they would live a life of enslavement like their parents. Some slaves worked in their master's house; these slaves had life easier than the slaves who worked on the field. There was often resistance to slavery by slaves during the transatlantic slave trade. There were times when slaves ran away from the plantations. Slaves also revolted and killed their masters and overseers. On many occasions, slave owners had to get backup to help them suppress the slave revolts. Once the slave master regained control of the situation, the leaders of the slave revolts that were captured were killed.

The Maroons were a group of Africans that escaped from slavery in Jamaica. The Maroons established their own self-sufficient communities on the island and they fought wars against the British in resistance to slavery. The Maroons won several battles against the British. The Maroons burned down plantations and helped slaves to escape. The Maroons were legally given status as freemen who were allowed to govern their own independent state after agreeing a treaty in 1739, that would end the feud between the British and the Maroons. But as a stipulation of the treaty they agreed, the Maroons had to return runaway slaves that had escaped from plantations and not get involved in future slave uprisings. The reason for slavery was economics. White slave owners wanted a free labour force to help them manufacture goods such as cotton, tobacco, rum and sugar. Once made, these goods were transported to Europe where the goods were exchanged for money. In 1776, America became independent. Britain's sugar colonies such as Jamaica and Barbados declined as America could trade directly with the French and Dutch in the West Indies. Furthermore, as the industrial revolution took hold in the 18th century; Britain no longer needed slave-based goods. The country was able to prosper from new systems which required high efficiency through free trade and free labour. Cotton rather than sugar became the main produce of the British economy and English towns such as Manchester and Salford became industrial centres of world importance.

Toussaint L'Ouverture led a successful slave revolt in Haiti. As a result of what happened, Haiti became the first independent black republic. The Haitian Revolution brought about ideas of liberty and equality amongst those who were seeking an end to slavery. Following the Haitian Revolution, there were many slave revolts across the Caribbean, which reduced the production and profitability of slavery. The slave revolts shocked the British government and made them see that the costs and dangers of keeping slavery in the West Indies were too high. In places such as Jamaica, many terrified plantation owners were ready to accept abolition rather than risk a widespread war.

When parliament was finally reformed in 1832, two-thirds of those who supported slavery were swept from power. The once powerful West India Lobby had lost its political strength. The demand for freedom for enslaved people had become almost universal. It was driven forward by the formal abolition campaign and by a coalition of non-conformist churches as well as Evangelicals in the Church of England. (Text in the last two paragraphs comes from the online article: Why was Slavery finally... abolished in the British Empire? The article was written by the Abolition Project and it is available from the web page: www.abolition.e2bn.org/slavery111.html. Accessed on 5 January 2018).

Slavery legally ended in the West Indies in August 1834. But slaves had to endure four years of apprenticeship, which was basically slavery but given a new name. The British government believed that apprenticeship would ease the transition from slavery to freedom, allow time for the formation of much of the social infrastructure of a free society, and prevent the collapse of the sugar estates by ensuring a continued supply of labour. But during the apprenticeship period, the mentality of the slave masters stayed the same; hence the conditions on the plantations remained the same. Even after the period of apprenticeship, some slave owners didn't tell the slaves they were free because the slave owners wanted to get more free labour out of the slaves. Slavery was a very profitable business for the privileged white society who were involved in the slave trade.

When the abolitionists demanded an end to slavery, the slave owners argued against ending slavery because of the financial loss they would suffer by freeing their slaves. In order to end slavery and appease the slave owners; the British government paid the slave owners financial compensation of £20 million (equivalent to £17 billion in money, as of 2015) altogether. But the slaves weren't given any compensation. So the slaves were left with no money, no land, no food, no jobs, and no assistance to help them support themselves.

POST-SLAVERY AND GARVEY

The legacy of slavery has left traumatic effects on the mental psyche of black people. The process of slavery had deprived black people of their freedom, language, culture and religious beliefs. Post-slavery, black people living in the Caribbean had a lack of racial self-esteem and they were missing an identity that defined who they were. Even though slavery ended, black people were still being treated inferior to white people in society. White people had more privileges than black people. The majority of the population in the Caribbean were black people but the majority of them were very poor. On the other hand, the small minority of the population were white but they were wealthy.

There was a Jamaican born man who had a mission to change the living conditions of black people around the world. This man was Marcus Garvey, Jamaica's first National Hero and founder of the Universal Negro Improvement Association and African Communities League (UNIA). The UNIA is an organisation that was formed to unite and empower black people across the world. The UNIA still exists today. Garvey travelled from Jamaica to America. He settled in New York, which is where he set-up the headquarters for the UNIA in 1917. Garvey and his UNIA established the Negro Factories Corporation, which had cooperative restaurants, steam laundry shops, tailor shops, dressmaking shops, millinery stores, a doll factory to manufacture black dolls, and a publishing house that produced a weekly newspaper. Garvey also established a steamship corporation, known as The Black Star Line. Garvey bought the ships with the intention to repatriate black people living in the diaspora back to Africa. The UNIA was in its prime during the mid-1920s when the organisation had millions of members that spread over more than forty countries, which included countries in the Americas, Europe, and Africa. Garvey enlightened people with his Pan-African teachings of racial pride, self sufficiency and nation building.

During slavery, the black slaves became Christians because Christianity was imposed on them by their slave masters. The slave owners used statements in the Bible to justify slavery. Leviticus 25:44-46: "You may purchase male or female slaves from among the foreigners who live among you. You may also purchase the children of such resident foreigners, including those who have been born in your land. You may treat them as your property, passing them on to your children as a permanent inheritance." The Bible was used to keep slaves submissive to their masters. In the Bible scripture Ephesians 6:5: "Slaves, obey your earthly masters with fear and trembling, with a sincere heart, as you would Christ."

Post-slavery, black people had a inferiority complex because for centuries they had been treated inferior to white people during slavery. Black people had also been brainwashed into thinking negatively about Africa. The image of God as a white man was in the minds of many black people. Jamaican black people admired the English royal family. People in Jamaica identified with Britain and the British monarchy because Jamaica was still a British colony until it gained independence in 1962 .

Garvey taught that black people should view God in their own image (as an African). On page 44 of the book *The Philosophy and Opinions of Marcus Garvey* (1986), Marcus Garvey stated: "If the white man has the idea of a white God, let him worship his God as he desires. If the yellow man's God is of his race let him worship his God as he sees fit. We, as Negroes, have found a new ideal. Whilst our God has no colour, yet it is human to see everything through one's own spectacles, and since the white people have seen their God through white spectacles, we have only now started out (late though it be) to see our God through our own spectacles. The God of Isaac and the God of Jacob let Him exist for the race that believes in the God of Isaac and the God of Jacob. We Negroes believe in the God of Ethiopia, the everlasting God — God the Father, God the Son and God the Holy Ghost, the One God of all ages. That is the God in whom we believe, but we shall worship Him through the spectacles of Ethiopia."

On page 184 of the book *Selected Writings and Speeches* of Marcus Garvey (2005), there is a reprint of an article written by Marcus Garvey, which was originally published in the Negro World Newspaper in 1925. In the article, Marcus Garvey wrote: "The time has come for the Negro to forget and cast behind him his hero worship and adoration of other races and to start out immediately to create and emulate heroes of his own... We must canonise our own saints, create our own martyrs, and elevate to positions of fame and honour black men and women who have made their distinct contributions to our racial history."

Marcus Garvey told black people to look to Ethiopia for a black God to identify with. On several speeches, Garvey preached the words from Psalms (68:32) in the Bible (King James Version) which states: "Princes shall come out of Egypt; Ethiopia shall soon stretch out her hands unto God." According to page 67 of Leonard E. Barrett's book *The Rastafarians* (1997), Marcus Garvey prophesied the coming of a back king in a speech in 1927. Barrett claims Garvey uttered the words: "Look to Africa for the crowning of a black king; he shall be the redeemer." Garvey wrote and produced a play, which was given the title *The Crowning of an Africa King*. The play was shown to an audience in Kingston, Jamaica in 1930. Towards the end of the play, there was a coronation of an African king.

THE EMERGENCE OF RASTAFARI AND LEONARD HOWELL

On 2 November 1930, Haile Selassie I was crowned Emperor of Ethiopia. His coronation ceremony took place in the Ethiopia capital Addis Ababa. The event was observed by a large crowd of Ethiopians, many of them had spent days or hours travelling to get to the event. There were also royal family members, head of states, and dignitaries from around the world who attended the coronation of Haile Selassie I.

At the time of Haile Selassie I's coronation, the majority of black people in the island of Jamaica were experiencing hard times. The British colonial government were in control of

Jamaica. Poverty was in abundance across the island. Black people were still suffering racial inferiority complexes even though slavery had legally ended almost a century ago. The majority of black Caribbean people had been brainwashed into thinking negatively about Africa because of European influences during slavery and colonialism. So Jamaican people didn't want to identify themselves as African. Jamaican people had British passports and they saw themselves as part of Britain. Jamaicans admired the British royal family. Most people in Jamaica were Christians. Christianity had a strong grip on the minds of the people. It was common for people to go church everyday and read the Bible daily.

Leonard Howell was a Garveyite and one of the founders of the Rastafari Movement. Howell was determined to liberate the minds of black people in Jamaica. Howell believed one of the biggest oppressors of black people had been Christianity. Howell denounced Christianity by claiming the religion to be a tool used by white people to keep black people down.

The Promised Key: The Original Literacy Roots of Rastafari (2001), is a book reintroduced by Ras E.S.P Mc Pherson. The book is a republication of the original document *The Promised Key*, which was written by Leonard Howell and published in 1935. On page 20 of *The Promised Key: The Original Literacy Roots of Rastafari*, Leonard Howell states: "The white man's doctrine (Christianity) has forced the black man to forsake silver and gold and seek Heaven after death. It has brought us to live in disgrace and die in dishonour. Now we the black man have found out that their doctrine was only a trick, and all their intention was to make themselves strong and to fool the black man."

Howell travelled through the streets of Jamaica and showed people he met a picture of Haile Selassie I. Howell would tell people that the person in the picture (Haile Selassie I) is their king and the ruler for black people. Howell detested the admiration that black people had for the British monarch, King George VI. Howell even told people that they should not pay taxes to King George VI.

On page 82 of the book *The Rastafarians* (1997), the author of the book Leonard E. Barrett highlighted what he believed to be the six principles of Rastafari, based on teachings from Leonard Howell at the time of 1933.

1. Hatred for the white race.
2. The complete superiority of the black race.

3. Revenge on whites for their wickedness.
4. The negation, persecution, and humiliation of the government and legal bodies of Jamaica.
5. Preparation to go back to Africa.
6. Acknowledging Emperor Haile Selassie I as the only ruler for black people.

Leonard Howell's teachings concerned the British colonial government in Jamaica. The government were worried that Howell's messages could destabilise the country and lead to an uprising. Howell was charged with sedition in 1934. Howell was imprisoned several other times during his life because of his black activism. Howell also spent time in Bellevue Mental Asylum because the authorities claimed he was a madman. Howell spoke to black people about the need to be self-reliant, so black people could build their own independent nation.

In 1941, Howell purchased five hundred acres of land in St. Catherine, Jamaica. The land was named Pinnacle and it became the safe haven for thousands of Rastafarians who lived and worked together in unity. Under Howell's leadership, Pinnacle became the most self-sufficient, economically empowered community in the island of Jamaica. Farmers lived and worked in Pinnacle. The farmers produced food for the people in the community to eat. Skilled craftsmen also lived and worked in Pinnacle. The craftsmen would teach others their skills. Ganja (also known as weed or marijuana) was grown and sold to the public to generate income. Ganja was also used for spiritual meditation or as a natural herb to heal people from illnesses. Howell use to give profits from the money made in Pinnacle to people that was suffering through poverty in the streets.

Pinnacle was raided several times by police on behalf of the government who were prejudice against Rastafarians. During the police raids, the police stole cash banked in Pinnacle. They also confiscated or burned the ganja. In 1958, Pinnacle was destroyed by police officers who were sent there by the government. The police raided the land, beat up the people and burned their houses down. The destruction of Pinnacle left the Rastafarians who lived there homeless. With little options, many Rastafarians moved to the Kingston slums, which included a place called Back-o-Wall; one of the poorest slums in Jamaica. In 1962, Back-o-Wall was demolished and between 1963-66, the land was redeveloped and renamed Tivoli Gardens.

PERSECUTION AGAINST RASTAFARI

People around the world often associate Jamaican culture with Rastafari. But Rastafari emerged as a subculture within the Jamaican society. Rastafari has faced a lot of persecution over the years by their fellow countrymen. There has always been a divide between the mainstream Jamaican society and Jamaican Rastafarians, whether it be for religious, cultural or political reasons. The majority population in Jamaica are Christians and it is Christians who have been at the forefront of a lot of the discrimination against Rastafarians in Jamaica.

The Jamaican government has also constantly tried to suppress the Rastafari Movement. Police use to harass Rastafarians and arrest innocent Rastafarians under false charges of possession

31

of ganja. Rastafarians had to be careful when travelling around in the streets because people from the public would verbally abuse them, attack them and try to cut off their dreadlocks. This forced Rastafarians to travel around in the gullies. Rastafarians would be refused to travel on airplane flights with their dreadlocks and beards. Businesses would not give jobs to Rastafarians because of their dreadlocks hairstyle or their beards. Rastafarians were even disowned by their own parents because their parents were Christians who held prejudice views about Rastafarians. The general biased view by the Jamaican public was that the Rastafarians were madmen, foolish, strange, dirty, and evil hearted.

The persecution against Rastafarians by the society is what caused many Rastafarians to relocate to live in secluded areas in the hills of Jamaica. In the DVD documentary *Bad Friday: Rastafari After Coral Gardens* (2011), Rastafarian Teddy "Silas" David said: "Rasta was like a species in Jamaica, they had to stay on the edge of society. We had to stay mostly in the hills. You couldn't venture too much into the cities and the towns; people didn't want to see you. If the police caught you with a little weed, and you go to jail and you are Rasta, the first thing the police do is cut off your locks." On the same documentary

Bad Friday: Rastafari After Coral Gardens, Selbourne Reid (a retired detective inspector of the police) mentioned the discrimination against Rastafarians by the Jamaican police. Reid said: "Rastafarians were not accepted as ordinary citizens. I recall in our shooting range, the targets were often times the image of a Rasta man with locks. In our mind, that was the look of a criminal."

Coral Gardens Massacre

On 12 April 1963, a group of Rastafarians where involved in an incident that began over a land dispute. Rudolph Franklyn was a Rastafarian who was farming on some land in Coral Gardens, near Montego Bay. When the land was sold to Ken Douglas, the new owner asserted his right to the property and attempted to drive the squatters off the land. As is often the case, the squatters refused to move. During one of several attempts at eviction, Franklyn was shot by the police. He survived but was told by a medical doctor that he would die soon because of the bullet lodged in his body by the police officer. Once Franklyn was released from hospital and then prison, he went to seek revenge with some of his associates who were also Rastafarians. Franklyn's group burned down a gas station in

Montego Bay. The gas station was owned by Ken Douglas. The gas station was burned down in the early hours of the morning on 12 April and by midday on the same day, Franklyn and seven other people had lost their lives.

Following the incident, Jamaica prime minister Sir Alexandra Bustamante turned all Rastafarians in Jamaica into villains. Bustamante ordered the police to beat Rastafarians, arrest them and kill them if necessary. Bustamante said: "Bring in all Rastas, dead or alive". The Rastafarians were hunted down by the police officers. Bustamante gave prosecution exemption to the police and members of the public for any assaults against Rastafarians during that period. Rastafarians were forcefully taken to prisons, packed next to each other in cells with little room to move and beaten up by the police. A victim of the Coral Gardens Massacre, claimed he was beaten up in front of Bustamante whilst in prison.

Despite the fact that the Rastafarians taken to prison hadn't committed any crimes to warrant their arrest, the Rastafarians were kept in prison until whenever the police officers wanted to release them. There were Rastafarians who spent months in prison for no reason or for made up charges by the police. Some Rastafari families were displaced. It is unknown the exact number of Rastafarians who were killed or injured as a result of the Coral Gardens Massacre because there were many unreported incidents.

Rastafarians commemorate the Coral Gardens Massacre every year. Since the tragedy of the Coral Gardens Massacre in 1963, Rastafarians have demanded that the Jamaican government be held accountable for the actions taken place in Coral Gardens. The Rastafarians have requested reparations from the Jamaican government to compensate for the loss of life of their members and for compensation to be given to those who suffered injuries as a result of the Coral Gardens Massacre. In 2017, the Jamaican prime minister Andrew Holness apologised on behalf of the government for the persecution against the Rastafari community, which was caused by the government during the Coral Gardens Massacre.

The Coral Gardens Massacre is an example of the strong division that existed in Jamaica between the Jamaican police, the society and the Rastafari community in Jamaica. It is strongly believed that if those involved in the group who burned the gas station down where not Rastafarians and they were another group such as Christians or Muslims; they would not have been subject to the persecution that Rastafarians faced. Bustamante used the Coral Gardens incident to give the police and the public an excuse so that they could brutalise Rastafarians, which was something that the police and the Jamaican public had wanted to do for a long time. The Coral Gardens Massacre showed how extremely prejudice Bustamante was towards Rastafarians because Bustamante persecuted all Rastafarians in Jamaica based on what a few Rastafarians had done, even though the actions of these men had nothing to do with their association to Rastafari.

THE RISE OF RASTAFARI

Despite the vicious efforts to stop Rastafari over the years by the Jamaican government and the public, Rastafari's popularity has grown in Jamaica and it has become generally accepted as a popular culture within the Jamaican society.

Speaking in the DVD *Roaring Lion: Rise of Rastafari* (2002), Filmore Alvaranga from Mystic Revelations said: "Today, when they see a Rasta man, it doesn't bother them, because there are so much of us now. They have got used to it because everywhere you go on the corner, you see a Rasta."

Views about Rastafari by the society has changed over the years. There is less persecution against Rastafari today, than there has been in previous decades. There are also fewer negative views about Rastafari today, in comparison to what people thought about Rastafarians during previous decades. People in Jamaican society today are sympathetic towards Rastafarians. People are gravitating towards Rastafari because they are unhappy with the lack of opportunities and poor state of affairs in Jamaica.

There a lot of young people who are turning away from the religion of Christianity and seeking something alternative to provide them with their spirituality. Rastafari gives people a form of spirituality, along with racial pride; an identity and a culture. Rastafari represents a voice for change; a change in the political system, a change in the way we live, and a change in the beliefs that our parents and grandparents taught us.

In 2013, the Rastafari group The Church of Haile Selassie I was given official religious status by the Jamaican government after failed attempts in previous years. In 2015, Jamaica's government passed the law to decriminalise ganja. The new law allows a person to keep up to 2 ounces of ganja on them, which enables the Rastafarians to smoke ganja for spiritual reasons. The change in law comes following decades of persecution from the police against the Rastafarians for possessing ganja, and decades of protests by Rastafarians to legalise the herb.

Today, Rastafari is a global phenomenon with

millions of followers who live around the world. There are even more Rastafarians that live outside of Jamaica than in Jamaica. There are many people who don't declare themselves with the name Rastafari but they have adopted parts of the Rastafati culture or ideology.

RASTAFARI BEYOND
THE BIBLE

What's key to understanding Rastafari theology is understanding that the Bible was not the initial inspiration behind Rastafari when it began in the 1930s. The true inspiration behind Rastafari was the Pan-African teachings of Marcus Garvey and the need for black people to define their own sense of spirituality. But when the Rastafari movement began in the early 1930s, Rastafarians were coming out of the Christian religion. These individuals were familiar with validating their belief system through text in the Bible. So despite converting to Rastafari from Christianity, many of the Rastafarians kept reading the Bible. But the Rastafarians interpreted the Bible in a different way than Christians. For example, many Rastafarians used scripture from the Bible as their reference point to validate Haile Selassie I to be the Lord God of Israel or the second coming of Jesus Christ.

Rastafarians adopted some culture from the Bible. For example, the dreadlocks hairstyle which was adopted from the Nazarenes, who were the followers of Jesus Christ. Another example of Rastafari adopting culture from the Bible, is the eating diet. Most Rastafarians don't eat meat or pork because the dietary laws in the Old Testament. The validation of Rastafari through the Bible is down to ignorance. In the past, Rastafari elders used the Bible because they didn't have much other sources of reference pertaining to Haile Selassie I or life in general. The Bible was the only book they knew that told them about a God and how to live. But now we're in the twenty first century we can get a much better understanding of life because there is more information and resources accessible to us. It is irrational for people to live a life based on the Bible because the book has flaws, lack of evidence, historical inaccuracies, unknown authors, and it was written by people who lived in a primitive time.

There are Rastafarians who hit out against the Bible and strongly oppose linking the Bible to Rastafari. Mutabaruka is a radio talk show host, dub poet and famous Rastafari elder, that has explained several times why Rastafari should stand on its own without reference to the Bible. On the website ireggae.com, there is an article written by Mutabaruka titled "A New Faculty of Interpretation". The article comes from the *8th Annual Reggae Festival Guide* (Available from: http://www.ireggae.com/newfaculty.htm. Last visited 15 January 2018). In the article "A New Faculty of Interpretation", Mutabaruka states: "When Rastafarians began the quest to find self, the only book that was available to us was the Bible and so the totality of what we understood to be true was based primarily on interpretation of this book. Even the idea of Haile Selassie as an African God was justified and validated by the Bible. We, as African people brought here from Africa under inhumane conditions, were forced to live - even now - without any kind of identity. This was also justified through the Bible by the European invaders and those Africans who sought to rationalize this enslavement by declaring that this was an act of God. The influence of this book runs deep. Over the years, Rastafarians declare themselves to be Israelites as referred to in the Old Testament, so that words and phrases such as Zion, Promised Land, the wicked Pharaoh and Jah became part of the language of the Rastafarian Movement.

We cannot continue to close out other information that is not in line with the Bible. The Bible is just one set of peoples' understanding of human behaviour and personality. The events recorded in the Bible are on the periphery of African knowledge. Stories recorded in the Bible have their genesis in other indigenous people's folk tales. What we are taking as history is other people's mythology. We will have to go beyond the Bible, we can no longer continue to justify Haile Selassie's divinity through the Davidic link. We can no longer be like Christian or Islamic fundamentalists - who are stuck in a history that does not provide them with an understanding of new thoughts and new life styles. Rastafari can only continue if we who profess this faith, understand that African philosophy and Africa spirituality cannot be bound into any book.

Our need to understand each other and our environment is very crucial in the rationalisation of our existence. This can only be realised through clarity of perception. Religion does not offer clarity. What religion offers is a perception and this perception comes through belief. This belief comes through faith and, as we know, faith is not knowledge. Faith is what we would like our perception to be or not to be. Rastafari must not be bound by religious perceptions because this will cause stagnation of the movement and create fundamentalism. We must be open to the different cultures of Africa and not demonise them because of biblical interpretations."

There is a strong link between slavery and the Bible. The first slave ship to take black people to the Caribbean was named *Jesus of Lubeck* (also called "The Good Ship Jesus"). The famous hymn *Amazing Grace* was written by John Newton, who was a slave owner. During the transatlantic slave trade, the Bible was used by white slave masters to justify slavery (Bible verses below and on the next page).

Leviticus 25:44-46 - "You may purchase male or female slaves from among the foreigners who live among you. You may also purchase the children of such resident foreigners, including those who have been born in your land. You may treat them as your property, passing them on to your children as a permanent inheritance."

Titus 2:9 - "Slaves are to be submissive to their own masters in everything; they are to be well-pleasing, not argumentative."

Ephesians 6:5 - "Slaves, obey your earthly masters with fear and trembling, with a sincere heart, as you would Christ."

Exodus 21:20-21 - "When a man strikes his slave, male or female, with a rod and the slave dies under his hand, he shall be avenged. But if the slave survives a day or two, he is not to be avenged, for the slave is his money."

Timothy 6:1 - "All who are under the yoke of slavery should consider their masters worthy of full respect, so that God's name and our teaching may not be slandered."

Timothy 6:2 - "Those who have believing masters should not show them disrespect just because they are fellow believers. Instead, they should serve them even better because their masters are dear to them as fellow believers and are devoted to the welfare of their slaves."

We cannot liberate our minds by using the Bible because the Bible was the book that was given to us by slaveholders four hundred years ago to keep us in bondage and submission. Instead, we must remember that there was an Africa that flourished thousands of years before we even heard of the name Jesus; there was an Africa where we built pyramids, an Africa that gave the world mathematics, an Africa that was advanced in science, and an Africa were some of us were kings and queens. African people have a glorious history and it's essential that our history is not forgotten about, especially by ourselves. We must not let Bible myths replace African history. Neither should we let the trials and tribulations that are ancestors faced to get us here be taken for granted. Many of our ancestors had no choice but to accept Jesus; we are now in a better position to understand how Christianity has been used as a tool to control our minds and pacify us.

Let's not forget, Christian missionaries went into Africa at the same time Europeans were carrying out their colonisation conquests in Africa. King Leopold II was responsible for the death of 10 million Africans in the Congo. He started his conquest of the Congo by introducing Christian missionaries. Under the instructions of King Leopold II, Congolese people were enslaved and forced to work to gather rubber. If they didn't meet their quota, they were murdered; mutilated or tortured. In South Africa, white Europeans stole the land from black people and the government imposed Apartheid law, which segregated white people from black people and gave white people all the privilege's in South Africa. Yet black people were taught to pray to the same Christian God and the same Jesus as the people oppressing them.

HAILE SELASSIE I - KING OF KINGS AND LORD OF LORDS

On 23 July 1892, Haile Selassie I was born in the Harar province of Ethiopia. His birth name was Tafari Wolde Mikael. Haile Selassie I's father was Ras Makonnen Wolde Mikael, the governor of Harar. Ras Makonnen Wolde Mikael's cousin was Emperor Menelik II. At the age of thirteen, Haile Selassie I became Deejazmatch (a title equivalent to that of Count) of the Harar province. A year later, his father died and he was looked after by his father's cousin, Menelik II.

In 1913, Menelik II died and Empress Zauditu took power. Haile Selassie I became regent, a position he stayed in for the next thirteen years. Haile Selassie I was known by the name Ras Tafari Makonnen during his time as regent. He helped to secure Ethiopia's entry into the League of Nations (now known as United Nations) in 1923. Haile Selassie I believed joining forces with members of the League of Nations would ensure collective security that would protect Ethiopia from colonialism. Ethiopia was the only African country in the League of Nations at the time of entering.

In 1928, Haile Selassie I was crowned King. Two years later, he became Emperor of Ethiopia on November 2, 1930. During his coronation, Haile Selassie I was given the titles: King of Kings, Lord of Lords, Conquering Lion of the Tribe of Judah, Elect of God, and Light of the World. Haile Selassie I's coronation was witnessed by thousands of spectators including dignitaries, representatives of governments, and royalty from across the world. At the time, Ethiopia and Liberia were the only two independent African countries. But Liberia didn't have a monarchy because it was a former colony of USA until 1847. So Haile Selassie I and Ethiopia became a symbol of black pride in Africa and throughout the African diaspora.

In 1935, the Italian Prime Minister Benito Mussolini declared war on Ethiopia. The fascist dictator wanted to take control of the only African country that had never been colonised. Mussolini wanted to build a powerful empire like

Ancient Rome. Italian troops invaded Ethiopia and killed over 200,000 Ethiopians during the war. Ethiopia and Italy were both members of the League of Nations. Italy breached the League of Nations treaty, which prohibited one nation from invading another nation who were also part of that same organisation. The Italians also used mustard gas to kill Ethiopians, even though mustard gas had been banned by international law for being too dangerous.

Haile Selassie I went to the League of Nations Geneva conference in Switzerland (1936) to make an appeal for help. But despite Haile Selassie I's plea for support to help Ethiopia in the war; no one offered to help Ethiopia. So with the Italians still occupying Ethiopia, Haile Selassie I went into exile in Bath, England.

In 1939, World War Two began between England and Germany. The Italians had become allies with the Germans in 1940. So England decided to join forces with the Ethiopians in the war against Italy because Ethiopia was being occupied by the Italians, who were England's enemies. In 1941, Haile Selassie I regained full control of Ethiopia, after English militants and Ethiopian troops combined defeated Italy in the war. Haile Selassie I became a hero in Ethiopia. But the war with Italy had left Ethiopia in a poor state. Many of the buildings, monasteries, and roads had been destroyed.

Haile Selassie I redeveloped Ethiopia by modernising the country. He helped establish Ethiopia's first airlines and he brought in skilled professionals from abroad to help rebuild Ethiopia. The foreign professionals helped with hospitals, schools, new buildings, and roadwork. Haile Selassie I played a key role in educating the people of Ethiopia. According to the obituary of Haile Selassie I on the New York Times website, 200 schools were formed between 1942 and 1952. (Available from: www.nytimes.com/learning/ general/onthisday/bday/0723.html. Accessed 15 January 2018). Haile Selassie I made himself Minister of Education. He even turned one of his palaces into a University. Haile Selassie I gave students money to buy school equipment.

In 1931, Haile Selassie I introduced Ethiopia's first constitution. This replaced the ancient laws of the Fetha Negast (Law of the Kings). Haile Selassie I's constitution reflected the modern times; slavery was made illegal and harsh punishment such as cutting off someone's hand for stealing was also made illegal in the country. In 1955, Haile Selassie I revised the constitution, which reflected more changes in legislation that was needed to modernise the country. But some

Ethiopians felt that he country was developing to slowly and that more reforms were needed in Ethiopia.

Whilst Haile Selassie I was visiting Brazil in 1960, rebels backed by the Imperial Guard and students from Haile Selassie I University, seized control of the Ethiopia capital Addis Ababa. The intent of the coup leaders was to establish a new government that would improve how the country was being run. But the coup failed because army and air force units remained loyal to Haile Selassie I, who returned to the capital on December 17, 1960. Many of the coup leaders were publicly executed. But their demands highlighted the growing dissatisfaction with Haile Selassie I's rule of governance by some of the Ethiopian public.

Haile Selassie I was a Pan-Africanist. In 1958, Haile Selassie I played a key role in establishing the United Nations Economic Commission for Africa (UNECA), which is a organisation that was established for the economic empowerment of African countries across the continent. The UNECA still exists today. It's headquarters remain in Ethiopia's capital Addis Ababa, where the organisation was initially set-up. In 1962, Selassie I founded the Organisation of African Unity (OAU) with the Ghana president Kwame

Nkrumah. The aim of the OAU was to unite African countries under one body to eradicate colonialism on the continent and for African countries to work together for the collective advancement of Africa. Haile Selassie I was selected as the first President of the OAU. Initially 36 countries were members of the OAU, but the number of African countries in the OUA has increased over the decades since it began. There are currently 54 African countries that are part of the African Union (which was renamed from the OAU in 2001).

Haile Selassie I supported the struggle against Apartheid in South Africa. In 1962, Nelson Mandela left South Africa in exile and he visited Ethiopia to get training by Haile Selassie I's military. During his stay, Mandela met with Haile Selassie I and Mandela informed Haile Selassie I about the situation in South Africa. On departure from Ethiopia, Haile Selassie I issued Mandela an Ethiopian passport with the alias name David Motsamayi. The passport was given to Mandela so he could return to South Africa (Mandela was wanted by the Apartheid regime during this time). Haile Selassie I also gave Nelson Mandela a handgun, so that Mandela could bring down the Apartheid government.

In 1948, Haile Selassie I donated 500 acres of

his own private land in Shashamane for black people living in the diaspora to repatriate to Africa. Rastafarians took the opportunity to move to Ethiopia but when Prime Minister Meles Zenawi took charge in 1995, Zenawi confiscated a large amount of the land and put the land in the control of the government. This partially caused the Rastafari population in Shashamane to decrease. At its peak, Shashamane was home to around 2,000 Rastafarians.

Haile Selassie I travelled around the world to countries in Africa, Europe, the Americas, the Caribbean, and the Middle East. He met with royalty and head of states of the countries he travelled to. Haile Selassie I received lots of accolades when he visited countries abroad. In 1954, Haile Selassie I revisited Bath in England; the place where he spent five years in exile during the Italian war with Ethiopia. Haile Selassie I was rewarded with the honour of being given the Freedom of the City (Bath). In 1965, Haile Selassie I went to the East African country Malawi and became the only head of state to visit the country.

Haile Selassie I received his best reception when he visited Jamaica in April 1966. There were thousands of people who gathered at the Norman Manley International Airport (formerly

Palisadoes Airport) to see Emperor Haile Selassie I. Protocol was broken down; people broke through the barriers and surrounded the plane to get a close look at Haile Selassie I. Rastafarian elder Mortimo Planno had to be brought to the plane to settle down the crowd. Rastafarians rejoiced in the presence of Haile Selassie I; the Rastafarians were singing and chanting. Haile Selassie I stayed in Jamaica for three days and he travelled to different parishes in the island. Ceremonies were held at various places during the time Haile Selassie I visited Jamaica. Haile Selassie I met with Rastafarians and he gave them medallions and told them to continue to spread Rastafari. Haile Selassie I said to them: "Organise and centralise". During Haile Selassie I's trip to Jamaica, he donated money to the Jamaican government for them to build a high school. Whilst in Jamaica, Haile Selassie I was awarded an honorary degree by the University of the West Indies. Haile Selassie I showed gratitude for the pleasant treatment that he received from Jamaicans during his stay in Jamaica by inviting the Jamaican government to become members of the Organisation of African Unity. Rastafarians celebrate April 21 every year to commemorate Haile Selassie I's visit to Jamaica. This day is known as Grounation Day.

Despite Haile Selassie I's popularity abroad, in Ethiopia people were becoming unhappy with the leadership of Haile Selassie I. Ethiopians were frustrated with the lack of finance in the country. People accused Haile Selassie I of embezzling government money and people from the more educated class, wanted the country to develop a lot quicker. The public started to question the capabilities of Haile Selassie I to govern the country because he was getting old. In 1973-74, there was a major drought which led to a famine. People in Ethiopia accused Haile Selassie I's government of neglecting the people suffering because of the famine. According to the Food and Agriculture Organisation report from the United Nations, 300,000 people died in Ethiopia's famine of 1973-74.

In September 1974, Mengistu Haile Mariam led a successful military coup against Haile Selassie I, which resulted in the removal of Haile Selassie I as ruler of the country. Mengistu Haile Mariam's regime took control of the country. Haile Selassie I was put under house arrest at the palace by orders of Haile Mariam. It was reported Haile Selassie I died in 1975. But the death surrounding Haile Selassie I is very controversial.

In 1975, news reports revealed that Haile

Selassie I died. In 1992, it was reported that Haile Selassie's remains were discovered, buried under a toilet in the Imperial Palace. Some Rastafarians reject the reports that Haile Selassie I died. In the 1990s, a cousin of Haile Selassie I was on Channel 4's television show *Devil's Advocate*, where he confirmed that Haile Selassie I died. But Rastafari activist Shango Baku denied the death of Haile Selassie I on the same show. (*Devil's Advocate*: www.youtube.com/watch?v=o9REza2jxUo. Accessed on 7 January 2018).

In March 2006, Master Yogiraj Siddhanath published his book Wings to Freedom. Master Siddhanath is a Guru who claims in his book that he met Haile Selassie I in 1982, which was seven years after it was reported that Haile Selassie I died. Siddhanath also mentions meeting Haile Selassie I's wife Empress Menen. But it is questionable how reliable Siddhanath's book is. If Siddhanath did meet Haile Selassie I, then it leads to several questions such as: did Haile Selassie I die after meeting Siddhanath or is Haile Selassie I still alive? If Haile Selassie I died after meeting Siddhanath, when exactly did Haile Selassie I die? Where did Haile Selassie I die? And how did Haile Selassie I die? Some Rastafarians believe that Haile Selassie I has made a mystical disappearance from the earth.

Regardless of the mystery surrounding his death, Haile Selassie I's place belongs in world history as a legend, who was one of the greatest monarchs to have ever ruled a country. Haile Selassie I was a strong leader who led by example. Haile Selassie I strove to modernise his country through introducing new developments of the 20th century, whilst trying to balance the customs and traditions of an ancient nation still living in the same ways to that of how their ancestors would have been living centuries ago. Haile Selassie I played a key role in building Ethiopia into what it is today. By introducing new developments to Ethiopia at the time, Haile Selassie I helped to lay down the foundation for the prosperity that Ethiopia is now benefiting from.

According to the World Bank's 2017 edition of Global Economic Prospects, Ethiopia was the second fastest growing economy in the world in 2017. (You can find this statement on the World Economic Forum web page via the link: www.weforum.org/agenda/2017/06/these-are-the-world-s-fastest-growing-economies-in-2017. Accessed on 12 January 2019). In 2018, CNN reported that Ethiopia was the fastest growing economy in Africa. The capital of Ethiopia is Addis

Ababa. The city Addis Ababa has experienced an average 10% economic growth each year over the last decade. (The last two statements comes from: www.edition.cnn.com/2018/04/24/africa/africa-largest-economy/index.html. Last visited the CNN web page on 12 January 2019).

REGGAE AND RASTAFARI

Reggae music has been crucial in promoting the message of Rastafari globally. In the 70s, reggae legend and Rastafari icon Bob Marley popularised reggae music and Rastafari through spreading the message of Rastafari around the world in his music. Bob Marley incorporated Rastafari messages in his songs.

In Bob Marley's song "Africa Unite" (1979), Bob Marley sang about the Rastafari principle of African unity. Bob Marley sang: "Africa unite: cause were moving right out of Babylon. How good and pleasant would it be before God and man, to see the unification of all Africans."

Bob Marley mentioned Rastafari messages in popular songs such as: "Rastaman Chant, Get Up Stand Up, Babylon System, Selassie is the Chapel, and Ride Natty Ride". Bob Marley died in 1981 but despite his death, Marley's popularity continued to grow. Reggae music stayed in the spotlight of Jamaican culture because the popularity of legendary reggae artists such as Gregory Isaacs, Burning Spear, Freddie McGregor, and Dennis Brown. Reggae became so popular, that tourists would visit Jamaica just to listen to reggae music and embrace in Rastafari culture. Today, reggae remains an important part of spreading Rastafari theology. You can hear the message of Rastafari in the songs of popular reggae artists such as Sizzla, Tarrus Riley, Jah Cure, Capleton, Richie Spice, Damien Marley, and Luciano.

In roots reggae music, you will hear words such as Babylon, Zion, or Jah. Those words are also used in the Bible but in Rastafari the meanings of those words have been altered. For example, Jah - the name given to Haile Selassie I, Zion - Africa, Babylon - white supremacy; a system of racism, oppression, materialism, capitalism and cultural imperialism, which is used to treat black people inferior to white people. Babylon can also refer to the Western world - a term used to define countries outside of Africa that's governments and societies have oppressed black people, particularly England, USA and Jamaica. In 1979, Bob Marley released a song called "Babylon System". Marley said in the song: "The Babylon system is a vampire, sucking the blood out of the children day by day."

The Rastafari principle of repatriation to Africa is spoken about in many reggae songs. In the song "Hurry Up and Come" by Cocoa Tea (1996), the artist said: "I home is not in Babylon, Mount Zion is I home… calling all Rastaman, no more will I and I roam… hurry up and come because Babylon done."

A classic reggae song is "Rivers of Babylon" by Brent Dowe and Trevor McNaughton of the Jamaican reggae group, The Melodians. The song was released in 1972. It was later revised by Boney M. in 1978. In the song "Rivers of Babylon" by Boney M., the group emphasises on the fond memories of Africa before the transatlantic slave trade. In the song, the group sang the lyrics: "By the rivers of Babylon, there we sat down, yeah, we wept, when we remembered Zion… Then the wicked carried us away, captivity, requiring of us a song… Now how shall we sing the Lord's song in a strange land?"

Reggae artists sing songs to give praise to Haile Selassie I. In 2011, Warrior King released his song, "All My Days". In the song, Warrior King said: "All my days, I'll be praising Ras Tafari… I love him for so many reasons, I'm inspired by his beautiful teachings."

THE PRESENCE OF
RASTAFARI IN ENGLAND

World War II ended in 1945. Following the war, England was in a poor state. Hundreds of thousands of English people died in the war. England needed a new labour force. People from the West Indies were invited by Queen Elizabeth II to come to England to help rebuild the country. There was a mass migration of West Indians moving to England between 1948-1970.

West Indians travelled to England in search of a better life than what they were experiencing in the Caribbean. So West Indians came to England with optimism and high spirits. The West Indian immigrants coming to England were made to believe that the streets of England were paved with gold. But when people from the West Indies arrived in England, they were subject to hostile treatment by the racist white society, which included the public and the police.

The West Indian immigrants and their children were subject to police brutality and public attacks by racist groups, such as the Teddy Boys and the National Front (NF). White English people in the society and politicians including Enoch Powell wanted the immigrants to leave the country. The West Indians were given low quality jobs, poor housing, poor schooling, and left marginalised by the majority white English society. Many landlords refused to rent a room to a black person. It was common to see writing on house doors, which stated: "No Blacks, No Dogs, No Irish". For those who immigrated to England from the West Indies, it was a far cry from what they expected England to be like and they were experiencing tough times.

In the 1970s, Rastafari became popular in England, particularly amongst black youths who were the children of the immigrants from the West Indies who were fed up with the oppressive white racist society "Babylon". Rastafarians rejected the submissive attitudes and Christian values of their parents. Rastafari attracted black youths who were marginalised by a Eurocentric educational system, alienated from mainstream society, and deemed ill-fitted for the labour market. Rastafarians promoted Black

Nationalism and repatriation to Africa.

The black youngsters took on the Rastafari philosophy because it promoted black pride and a and a way of protesting against racism. The children of the West Indian immigrants had a lack of identity because they weren't born in the West Indies like their parents; they were born and bred in England. But the black youths couldn't identify themselves as English because England was a racist country that hated black people. Rastafari appealed to black youths because it gave them an alternative way to define themselves. Rastafari gave them a Pan-African identity that even their parents from the Caribbean were missing.

Reggae legend and Rastafarian Peter Tosh spoke about the Rastafari perspective of identity in his song "African" (1977). In the song, Tosh sang the lyrics: "Don't care where you come from, as long as you're a black man, you're an African, no mind your nationality, you have got the identity of an African."

Rastafari has played a key role in educating black people about the history of Africa pre-slavery. Dr William 'Lez' Henry is a community activist, academic, writer, and public speaker. In an interview, Dr William 'Lez' Henry recalled growing up during the 70s and 80s in England.

Dr William 'Lez' Henry said: "Going to school in the UK like I did, and even now, children are taught very little, hardly anything of note, about the African contribution to civilization or even a viable and historical African presence pre-slavery. When we were taught this by a Rastafarian or other people like Professor Gus John, it blew our minds. We would be like, "hold on a second," because all we were taught is that we were smiling slaves. That we were savages taken from Africa, civilized in the Caribbean by the whip or whatever, and now here we are, where we should be grateful to Europe. And then you get another history where you realize there was a viable African presence thousands of years before Europe or Europeans knew what it was to be civilized. That's truth! For a lot of people, it doesn't sit right for them but those are the kind of knowledge that we got from Rastafari." (Interview with Dr William 'Lez' Henry available from the webpage: www.pri. org/stories/2014-02-13/interview-dr-william-lez henry-racism-uk-rastafari-and-transcendent-natu re-sound. Accessed on 21 January 2018.)

Rastafari is not as popular amongst today's youths in England compared to how it was in the 70s and 80s when Rastafari was at its peak in England. But there are still Rastafari groups and individuals that are influential to black communities in England. In 2015, Rastafari Movement UK was one of the groups that helped to organise and participate in a march for slavery reparations to be given to people of African heritage because of the role Britain played in the transatlantic slave trade. The march was carried out through the streets of London. There were thousands of people that attended the event. Reparations activist Esther Stanford (supported by Rastafarians with her), delivered a petition for reparations to the government officials at 10 Downing Street.

MUTABARUKA - THE CUTTING EDGE

Mutabaruka is a radio talk show host, dub-poet, musician, actor, journalist, public speaker, and Rastafari icon. He has travelled around the world propagating the message of Rastafari. Mutabaruka is known as one of the leading exponents of the Rastafari Movement. Mutabaruka was born on December 26, 1952 in Kingston, Jamaica. His birth name is Allan Hope. But he later adopted the nickname Mutabaruka from the Rwandan poet Jean-Baptiste Mutabaruka.

Mutabaruka was raised as a Christian but converted to Rastafari during his teenage years. At school, Mutabaruka developed further black awareness. He had the privilege of being taught by Marcus Garvey Junior at Kingston Technical High School. Mutabaruka read books such as

The Autobiography of Malcolm X and other black educational books which were banned in Jamaica at the time.

Mutabaruka is the presenter of radio talk show *The Cutting Edge*. On his radio talk show, Mutabaruka talks about a wide range of topics. These topics include black consciousness, history, religion, politics, sexism, and current affairs. Some of the most notable guests to have featured on his radio show include Minister Louis Farrakhan, Runoko Rashidi, Ray Hagins, Bunny Wailer, and Capleton. Mutabaruka interacts with the audience on his show by discussing topics with listeners who call-in to talk on the show. *The Cutting Edge* show is broadcasted weekly and the show is also very popular outside of Jamaica.

In England, fans of *The Cutting Edge* stay up through early hours of the morning to listen to the show. Fans also listen to broadcasts of *The Cutting Edge* on YouTube. Even after two decades of *The Cutting Edge*, the show is still flourishing. Due to the huge success of *The Cutting Edge*, IRIE FM radio station decided to give Mutabaruka more airtime on IRIE FM. In 2013, Mutaburuka started hosting his second show on IRIE FM. The show is called the *Steppin Razor* and it is broadcasted every Thursday on IRIE FM. *Steppin Razor* is a radio talk show, like *The Cutting Edge*.

Mutabaruka has caused a lot of controversy because of his views on religion. Mutabaruka featured on the documentary *Coping with Babylon* (2007), where he explained why he believes Christianity has had a negative influence on Rastafari. Mutabaruka said: "Christianity does not allow you to accept other cultures that are not inclined with Christianity. Because we have maintained that Christian mind-set, it has not allowed us to accept African retentions." Mutabaruka has been a guest on three TV episodes of *Religious Hardtalk* hosted by Ian Boyne. On each show, Mutabaruka denounced Christianity.

During the 1980s and 1990s, Mutabaruka released several albums, which included *Check It* (1983), *The Mystery Unfolds* (1986), *Any Which Way... Freedom* (1989), *Melanin Man* (1994) and *The Ultimate Collection* (1996). Mutabaruka published *The First Poems* poetry book in 1980. A sequel poetry book called *The Next Poems* was released in 2005. Mutabaruka featured on Def Poetry Jam, with his popular poem called "Dis Poem". As an actor, Mutabaruka won plaudits for his performance as Shango in Haile Gerima's film *Sankofa* (1993).

Several times Mutabaruka has mentioned that

Rastafari should get more recognition from the Jamaican society. Onstage at Emancipation Park in Jamaica (2007), Mutabaruka delivered a speech where he demanded more respect to be given to Rastafarians. He said: "The amount of things Rasta do for Jamaica, you should respect us more because we get the most persecution in Jamaica. If it wasn't for Rasta, Jamaica would not be known like how Jamaica is known overseas. The words of Rastafari put Marcus Garvey in the school. It is the voice of Rastafari that put Emancipation Day back on the calendar. Its Rastafari culture (why) tourists come here (Jamaica). And overseas, its Rastafari that draw thousands of people to a music named reggae music." (Mutabaruka's speech was taken from the YouTube web page: www.youtube.com/ watch?v=2sV8zvh_EZg. Accessed on 21 January 2018).

RASTAFARI DAYS OF CELEBRATIONS

6 February – Bob Marley Birthday

A day to honour the life and legacy of reggae legend and Rastafari icon Bob Marley. Marley is the most famous Rastafarian and he has played a crucial role in spreading the Rastafari Movement worldwide through his songs of liberation and his powerful speeches of wisdom.

21 April – Grounation Day

On the 21 April 1966, Emperor Haile Selassie I visited Jamaica. It was the first and only time Haile Selassie I visited Jamaica; the country where the Rastafari Movement began. During Haile Selassie I's visit, he met with Rastafarians and he gave them medallions. Rastafarians who met Haile Selassie I, claim Selassie I told them to continue what they were doing by propagating the Rastafari Movement. On Haile Selassie I's trip to Jamaica, Selassie I also donated money to help the Jamaican government build a school and he invited Jamaica to become a member of the Organisation of African Unity.

16 June – Leonard Howell Birthday

On this day, Rastafarians honour the life and legacy of Leonard Percival Howell. This man was the most known preacher of Rastafari amongst the early founders of Rastafari. Howell was an outspoken leader who detested the British monarchy and he tried to steer black people away from Christianity.

23 July – Haile Selassie I Birthday

On this day, Rastafarians celebrate the life and legacy of Haile Selassie I. Rastafarians regard Haile Selassie I as a messiah who came to free them from colonialism and guide them back to their ancestral land Africa after 400 years of living in exile in the Western World (Babylon).

17 August – Marcus Garvey Birthday

On this day, Rastafarians honour the life and legacy of their prophet Marcus Mosiah Garvey. In the 1920s, Garvey prophesied the coming of an

African king to liberate black people from white supremacy. Rastafari is based on Garvey's Pan-African teachings. Leonard Howell was a former member of Marcus Garvey's Universal Negro Improvement Association. Rastafarians have been at the forefront in spreading Garvey's teachings.

11 September – Ethiopia New Year

Ethiopia new year begins on 11 September. A year in the Ethiopian calendar is 13 months long, with 12 months of 30 days each. The last month has 5 days in a common year and 6 days during leap year. Like in the Julian calendar, a leap year in the Ethiopian calendar happens every 4 years without exception.

2 November – Coronation of Haile Selassie I as Emperor of Ethiopia

On this day in 1930, Haile Selassie I was crowned as Emperor of Ethiopia. Following the coronation of Haile Selassie I, Leonard Howell started preaching that Emperor Haile Selassie I is the black messiah.

BIBLIOGRAPHY

Books

Adams, N., 2002. *A Historical Report: The Rastafari Movement in England.* London: GWA Works.

Barrett, L., 1997. *The Rastafarians.* USA: Beacon Press.

Biblica, 1978. *Holy Bible: New International Version.* USA: Biblica.

Garvey, A., 1986. *The Philosophy & Opinions of Marcus Garvey, or Africa for the Africans.* Dover, Massachusetts: Majority Press.

Garvey, M., 2005. *Selected Writings and Speeches of Marcus Garvey.* USA: Dover Publications.

Howell, L., 2001. *The Promised Key: The Original Literary Roots of Rastafari.* Brooklyn, New York. A&B Publishers Group.

John, D., 2010. *A Black History of Southampton: 16th Century to 21st Century.* Southampton, England: Positive Message Limited.

King, S., 2002. *Reggae, Rastafari, and the Rhetoric of*

Sandford, C., 1999. *The Lion of Judah Hath Prevailed: Being an Authorized Biography of H.I.M.*

Haile Selassie I. Research Associates School Times. Distribution International.

Siddhanath, Y., 2004. *Wings to Freedom*. 1st ed. USA: Alight Publications.

Thompson, D., 1999. *The Pan-Africanists*. Jamaica: Ian Randle Publishers.

Ullendorf, E., 1999. *Autobiography of Haile Selassie I Volume 1, My Life and Ethiopian Progress*.

Research Associates School Times Publications and Frontline Distribution International.

Usry, G. & Keener, C., 1996. *Black Man's Religion: Can Christianity Be Afrocentric?* Illinois, USA: InterVarsity Press.

Watch Tower Bible and Tract Society of Pennsylvania, 1961. *New World Translation of the Holy Scriptures*. USA: Watch Tower Bible and Tract Society of Pennsylvania.

DVD

Bad Friday: Rastafari After Coral Gardens, 2011. [DVD] Deborah A. Thomas and John L. Jackson, Jamaica: Oxumgirl Productions.

Coping with Babylon: The Proper Rastology, 2007. [DVD] Oliver Hill, Jamaica: Sonerito.

Fire in Babylon, 2011. [DVD] Stevan Riley. Revolver Entertainment.

Holding on to Jah, 2011. [DVD] Roger Hall and Harrison Stafford, Jamaica: Groundation Films and Infinite Mind Media.

Marley, 2012. [DVD] Kevin MacDonald, Jamaica: Magnolia Home Entertainment.

Motherland, 2010. [DVD] Owen Alik Shahadah, USA: Halaqah Films.

Roaring Lion: The Rise of Rastafari, 2002. [DVD] Ishmahil Blagrove, Jamaica: Rice N Peas.

Online Video

616blabla. (2012). *H.I.M. Haile Selassie, the Lion of Judah (full documentary)*. [Online Video]. 24 June 2012. Available from: ww.youtube. com/watch?v=75 GQ3rwxtZI. [Accessed: 7 January 2018].

Backpack Director. (2012). *Rastamentary*. [Online Video]. 1 November 2012. Available from ww.youtube.com/watch?v=LY28Hchq9xk [Accessed: 15 January 2018].

BBC (2015). *Britain's Forgotten Slave Owners S01 E02 The Price Of Freedom Official*. [Online Video]. 15 January 2018. Available from:

ww.youtube.com/watch?v=kg aJyp8ix4M. [Accessed: 18 January 2018].

BBC. (2015). *The Windrush Years 3*. [Online Video]. Available from: www.dailymotion.com/ video/x2 m7m8w. [Accessed: 7 January 2018].

Bro. Ldr. Mbandaka. (2016). *Garvey, Selassie & Rastafari - Countering the Conspiracy To Destroy this Epiphany!* [Online Video]. 29 April 2016. Available from: www.youtube. com/watch?v=v10OOlhL7SM. [Accessed: 15 January 2018].

Catherine Howell. (2013). *FROM PINNACLE TO SHASHEMANE*. [Online Video]. 2 January 2013. Available from: https://www.you tube.com/watch?v=fWN-7orHy3k. [Accessed on 15 January 2018].

Claude Sinclair. (2018). *MUTABARUKA RIPS EMANCIPATION PARK @ TRIBUTE TO MARCUS GARVEY 2ND EDITION 2012*. [Online Video] 4 September 2012. Available from: https://www.youtube.com/watch? v=2sV8zvh_EZg [Accessed 8 April 2018].

CGTN Africa. (2014). *Faces of Africa - Haile Selassie: The pillar of Ethiopia, part 1 & 2*. [Online Video]. 18 July 2014. Available from:

ww.youtube.com/watch?v=bV ki9t3anJU. [Accessed: 7 January 2018].

CGTN Africa. (2014). *Faces of Africa: Rastafarians coming Home to Africa*. [Online Video]. 7 July 2014. Available from: ww.youtube.com/watch?v=H Q6uGRmPQSQ. [Accessed: 7 January 2018].

Daily Alternative News. 2013. *Bob Marley New Zealand Interview 1979*. [Online Video]. 6 March 2013. Available from: www.youtube.com/watchv=Uj2JQWhiF0. [Accessed 15 January 2018].

Channel 4 "Devil's Advocate". *Debate on Divinity of HIM Haile Selassie I*. [Online Video]. 19 November 2012. Available from: www.youtube.com/watch?v=o9REza2jxU. [Accessed: 7 January 2018].

Nickele Morgan. (2013). *The meaning of Marcus Garvey to Rastafari Documentary*. [Online Video]. 16 March 2013. Available from ww.youtube.com/watch?v=IyCqmP4dE4M. [Accessed: 15 January 2018].

Ras Kwadwo. (2013). BAD FRIDAY, RASTAFARI & REPARATIONS – Ras Kwadwo (Pt1). [Online Video]. 12 September 2013.

Available from www.youtube.com/watch? v=imBRAGpYPwE. [Accessed 8 January 2018].

Ras Kwadwo. (2013). BAD FRIDAY, RASTAFARI & REPARATIONS - Ras Kwadwo (Pt2). [Online Video]. 12 September 2013. Available from www.youtube.com/watch? v=urzawDtm_Q. [Accessed: 15 January 2018].

Radio Shows

Alkebulan Revivalist Movement, 2016 [Radio]. *Afrika Speaks with Alkebulan: Groundation at 50, Where is Rastafari Today? Part 1, Galaxy Radio*. 18 April. 20.00.

Alkebulan Revivalist Movement, 2016 [Radio]. *Afrika Speaks with Alkebulan: Groundation at 50, Where is Rastafari Today? Part 2, Galaxy Radio*. 25 April. 20.00.

Website Articles

Alden Whitman. "Haile Selassie of Ethiopia Dies at 83". [Online] Available from http:// www.nytimes.com/learning/general/onthisday/ bday/0723.html. [Accessed 15 January 2018].

CNN. 2019. Ethiopia is now Africa's fastest growing economy. [ONLINE] Available from https://edition.cnn.com/2018/04/24/africa/africa-largest-economy/index.html. [Accessed 6 January 2019].

Dr. William 'Lez' Henry. 2014. "Interview: Dr. William 'Lez' Henry on Racism in the UK, Rastafari and Transcendent Nature of Sound Systems". [ONLINE] Available from: www.pri.org/stories/2014-02-13/interview-dr-william-lez-henry-racism-uk-rastafari-and-transcendent-nature-sound. [Accessed 21 January 2018].

Jamaica Woman Tongue. 2013. 'Bring In All Rastas, Dead Or Alive!'. [ONLINE] www.carolynjoycooper.wordpress.com/2013/0407/bring-in-all-rastas-dead-or-alive. [Accessed 6 January 2019].

King's College London. "The Apprenticeship System". [ONLINE] Available at: http://www.kingscollections.org/exhibitions/specialcollections/caribbean/experiment/apprenticeshipsystem. [Visited 15 January 2018].

Mutabaruka. "A New Faculty of Interpretation". [ONLINE] Available from: http://www.

ireggae.com/newfaculty.htm. Last visited on 15 January 2019).

The Abolition Project. 2010. "Why was Slavery finally abolished in the British Empire?". [ONLINE] Available from https://www. abolition.e2bn.org/slavery_111.html. [Accessed 15 January 2018].

World Economic Forum. 2017. "World Economic Forum. 2017. These are the world's fastest-growing economies in 2017. [ONLINE] Available from: https://www.weforum. org/agenda/2017/06/these-are-the-world-s-fastest-growing-ecnomomies-in-2017-2. [Accessed 6 January 2019].

ABOUT THE AUTHOR

Makonnen Sankofa is a devout Rastafarian and a Pan-African activist. Makonnen is a member of the Luton Black Men Community Group. One of the aims of the group is to provide solutions to issues that are affecting black communities. Another aim of Luton Black Men Community Group is to help those in the group improve their leadership skills. Luton Black Men Community Group host a wide variety of events throughout the year. These events include film screenings, lectures and seminars. Makonnen is also a member of African Heritage Network of Luton, which is a community group that host Kwanzaa celebration events every year. Makonnen is an ex-member of the interim National Afrikan People's Parliament, which was a political organisation that was formed to help preserve, protect and promote the best interests of African people living in the UK.

Makonnen has accomplished a lot with his black activism. Makonnen has won two debating contests that were hosted by Diaspora Debating Association. The debates Makonnen won, were based on topics effecting black communities in England. In 2018, Makonnen presented his own video clip that featured on BBC Three to help promote the awareness of Kwanzaa. In 2016, Makonnen wrote the winning essay which helped his friend and colleague Bevis Gooden from Luton Black Men Community Group win the Luton and Bedfordshire Community Awards Volunteer of the Year Award. During the same year, Makonnen was invited to speak to David Cameron (prime minister at the time) about the European Union referendum on ITV's European Union referendum debate shown on ITV 1.

Makonnen graduated from university with a Bachelor of Arts (BA Hons) degree in Sports Journalism. He learned about the history of West Indian cricket during his time studying the course. Makonnen enjoyed learning about West Indian cricket. He was especially interested in the subject because he supports West Indies cricket team, he use to play cricket when he was a child, and he has West Indian ancestry. Makonnen wrote an article about the history of West Indies cricket, which was published in *Jus Jah* Rastafari magazine. In 2013, Makonnen donated money to Jamaica Rastafarian Development Community School, which is a self-funded school that provides education to four hundred children in Ethiopia. Makonnen has also donated money to Pan-African organisations to help them continue with their work.

Born Matthew Berbeck, Makonnen legally changed his name to Makonnen Sankofa due to the strong influence of Rastafari and his black consciousness. Makonnen decided to change his name because he wanted to have a name that reflected his identity. He decided to name himself Makonnen because of his association with Rastafari and his admiration of Haile Selassie I. Haile Selassie I's name was Ras Tafari Makonnen, before he became the Emperor of Ethiopia. Makonnen chose the surname Sankofa because the meaning of the word. Sankofa means to go back, study and learn from the past so you are better equipped to move forward in the future. The word Sankofa originates from the Akan people of Ghana. Many of the people from the Akan tribe where taken from Ghana and brought to the West during the transatlantic slave trade. A subgroup of the Akan tribe is the

Ashanti (Asante). In the 17th and 18th century, the Ashanti Empire was the most powerful kingdom in Ghana and one of the most powerful kingdoms in the world. The Ashanti Empire was very wealthy and the leaders of the Ashanti had a lot of Gold. The Ashanti people are known for producing a unique material that is named kente cloth.